Welcome to
SPRINGFIELD

This edition published in 2023 by OH!
An Imprint of Welbeck Non-Fiction Limited,
part of Welbeck Publishing Group.
Offices in: London – 20 Mortimer Street, London W1T 3JW
and Sydney – Level 17,207 Kent St, Sydney NSW 2000 Australia
www.welbeckpublishing.com

ISBN 978-1-80069-525-2

Compiled and written by: David Clayton
Editorial: Victoria Denne and Malcolm Croft
Project manager: Russell Porter
Design: Tony Seddon
Production: Jess Brisley

A CIP catalogue record for this book is available from the British Library

Printed in China

10 9 8 7 6 5 4 3 2 1

Welcome to SPRINGFIELD

THE LITTLE GUIDE TO
THE SIMPSONS
UNOFFICIAL AND UNAUTHORIZED

CONTENTS

INTRODUCTION

With its 34th season starting in September 2022, *The Simpsons'* popularity shows no sign of waning. One of television's longest-running and most successful series, the animated adventures of the dysfunctional family from Springfield, USA will have reached an incredible landmark of 750 episodes by the end of the latest season.

Not bad for an idea that was sketched in a hallway ahead of a pitch meeting with producer James L. Brooks!

Creator Matt Groening couldn't have imagined that his idea would not only win a five-minute slot on *The Tracey Ullman Show* but go on to become commissioned as a half-hour prime-time show and ratings success.

Though there had been other dysfunctional US families on TV, such as the 1950s favourite *Father Knows Best* (not coincidentally also set in Springfield, Anywhere, USA) and the 1970s family comedy *Wait Till Your Father Gets Home* – which, incidentally, also started life as a short, animated segment on a prime-time show.

The Simpsons centres around the world of Homer and Marge Simpson and their children, Bart, Lisa and Maggie.

The family, despite their longevity, never age and Springfield provides the backdrop for the family's many adventures, with the American town providing a shifting landscape to suit all storylines.

While the Simpson family are central to all episodes, a large and eclectic cast of characters ensure that there are numerous continuing threads that connect each episode, from the god-fearing Flanders family who have the misfortune to live next door to the Simpson clan, to local bar owner Moe, Comic Book Guy and many, many others.

The Simpsons are part of popular culture across the world, adored by millions with phrases that have become part of everyday life in America and around the globe.

The *Simpsons* is a phenomenon, the like of which we may never see again…

Long may it continue.

CHAPTER
ONE

HOMER'S WORDS OF WIS-*D'OH*-M

There's more to Homer Simpson than just his crackpot schemes and *Duff*-addled parenting. He is the show's greatest weapon to demonstrate the flaws in the American Dream – as well as the contradictions at the heart of the nuclear American family.

The classic middle-class anti-hero, Homer is the perfectly imperfect vessel to reveal these traditional values for what they *really* are.

"D'oh!"

Homer's catchphrase – modelled by
voice actor Dan Castellaneta on the "d'oh!"
expressed by Jimmy Finlayson, the
Scottish actor who appeared in
33 Laurel and Hardy films.

As heard on almost every episode of The Simpsons…

You don't win friends with salad.

Homer *advises daughter Lisa he will be less popular if he hosts meat-free BBQs!*

As seen on Screenrant's Best Quotes from *The Simpsons* (Season 7, Episode 5, "Lisa The Vegetarian")

The Simpsons was conceived by Matt Groening shortly before a pitch for a series of animated shorts with producer James L. Brooks. Groening created a dysfunctional family and named the characters after his own family members.

A series of shorts was commissioned and became part of *The Tracey Ullman Show*, airing for the first time on April 19, 1987.

You can have all the money in the world, but there's one thing you will never have... a dinosaur.

Never a truer word...

As seen on Reddit's *Simpsons* Quotes for Every Day

"

To alcohol! The cause of, and solution to, all of life's problems.

"

__Homer__ fights against prohibition and celebrates the double-edged sword that is also one of his favourite hobbies… drinking.

As seen on Screenrant's Best Quotes from *The Simpsons* (Season 8, Episode 18, "Homer vs. The Eighteenth Amendment")

A boy without mischief is
like a bowling ball without a
liquid center.

Homer – *prepared to accept his son's many
misdemeanours.*

As seen on Simpsons.Fandom.com
(Season 1, Episode 8, "The Tell-Tale Head")

Bart, a woman is like beer. They look good, they smell good, and you'd step over your own mother just to get one!

*Fatherly advice from **Homer** to his son…*

As seen on Simpsons.Fandom.com

Marriage is like a coffin and each kid is another nail.

Homer's *simplistic and slightly off-putting view on marital life.*

As seen on the *Telegraph's* Best 40 *Simpsons* Quotes (Season 14, Episode 2, "How I Spent My Strummer Vacation")

What's the point of going out?
We're just gonna wind up back
home anyway.

*Homebird **Homer's** reluctance to leave his
home comforts – namely a couch, TV, and
beer – for too long, surfaces on a stripped-
back look at days out with the family.*

As seen on the *Telegraph's* 40 Best *Simpsons* Quotes

Son, if you really want something in this life, you have to work for it. Now, quiet! They're about to announce the lottery numbers.

Nobody does mixed messages like
Homer Simpson...

As seen on the *Telegraph's* 40 Best *Simpsons* Quotes

A feature-length film, *The Simpsons Movie*, was released in theatres worldwide on July 27, 2007 and grossed over $527 million.

The series has also spawned numerous comic book series, video games, books and other related media, and a billion-dollar merchandising industry.

Kids, you tried your best and you failed miserably. The lesson is, never try.

Homer *delivers one of the life lessons he's learned and accepted and urges his children to follow his advice.*

As seen on Simpsons.Fandom.com (Season 2, Episode 7, "Bart vs. Thanksgiving")

It takes two to lie; one to lie, and one to listen.

*Quintessential **Homer Simpson**...*

As seen on Screenrant's Best Quotes from *The Simpsons* (Season 3, Episode 20, "Colonel Homer")

Kids are great. You can teach them to hate what you hate and, with the internet and all, they practically raise themselves.

Homer's guide for modern parenting...

As seen on *The Scotsman's* 100 of Homer Simpson's Most Stupidly Hilarious Quotes

When Matt Groening was
creating the Simpsons,
he wanted them to stand out.

An animator came up with
the Simpsons' yellow and as
soon as she showed it to me
I said: "This is the answer!"
because when you're flicking
through channels with
your remote control, and a
flash of yellow goes by,
you'll know you're watching
The Simpsons.

It's so simple to be wise... just think of something stupid to say and then don't say it.

Simple advice we can all follow...

As seen on Screenrant's Best Quotes from *The Simpsons*

"

I want to share something with you: The three little sentences that will get you through life. Number 1: Cover for me. Number 2: Oh, good idea, Boss! Number 3: It was like that when I got here.

"

Homer's *tips for any situation…*

As seen on Screenrant's Best Quotes from *The Simpsons*

“

I think the saddest day of my life was when I realized I could beat my dad at most things, and Bart experienced that at the age of four.

”

__Homer__ reflects on four happy years…

As seen on *Irish Examiner's* Wit and Wisdom of Homer Simpson (Series 1, Episode 6, "Moaning Lisa")

I'm not a bad guy. I work hard and I love my kids... so why should I spend half my Sunday hearing about how I'm going to hell?

Homer *argues against regular church attendance.*

As seen on *Irish Examiner's* Wit and Wisdom of Homer Simpson (Season 4, Episode 3, "Homer the Heretic")

Oh, and how is education supposed to make me feel smarter? Besides, every time I learn something new, it pushes some old stuff out of my brain. Remember when I took that home winemaking course and I forgot how to drive?

Homer argues he's learned all he can…

As seen on Screenrant's Best Quotes from *The Simpsons* (Series 5, Episode 22, "Secrets of a Successful Marriage")

Why do you need new bands? Rock and roll attained perfection in 1974. It's a scientific fact!

Homer *argues music has not progressed much over the years…*

As seen on Screenrant's Best Quotes from *The Simpsons* (Season 7, Episode 24, "Homerpalooza")

If God didn't want me to eat chicken in church, then he would have made gluttony a sin.

Homer – *not au fait with the seven deadly sins…*

As seen on I-News' Best *Simpsons* Quotes

When someone tells you your butt is on fire, you should take them at their word.

Sound advice we can all follow!

As seen on *Esquire*'s "Homer Simpson: What I've Learned"

> 66
>
> There is no such thing as
> a bad donut.
>
> 99

This is an unproven statement…

As seen on *Esquire*'s "Homer Simpson: What I've Learned"

66

If you want results, press the red button. The rest are useless.

99

*A **Homer** tip that has more than a grain of truth…*

As seen on *Esquire's*, "Homer Simpson: What I've Learned"

There are many different religions in this world, but if you look at them carefully, you'll see that they all have one thing in common. They were invented by a giant, super-intelligent slug named Dennis.

Dennis has so much to answer for!

As seen on *Esquire*'s "Homer Simpson: What I've Learned"

There are way too many numbers. The world would be a better place if we lost half of them – starting with 8. I've always hated 8.

As seen on Esquire's "Homer Simpson: What I've Learned"

Oh, God gets your prayers,
but he just clicks delete without
reading them...

Homer's *prayers clearly end up in the recycle
bin on a regular basis…*

As seen on Screenrant's Best Quotes from *The Simpsons*
(Season 26, Episode 16, "Sky Police")

I never ate an animal I didn't like.

Homer's basic rule of being a carnivore.

As seen on *Esquire*'s, "Homer Simpson: What I've Learned"

Lord help me, I'm just not
that bright.

*Being comfortable with his own limitations
has never been an issue for **Homer**...*

(Season 1, Episode 13,"Some Enchanted Evening")

A fool and his money are soon parted. I would pay anyone a lot of money to explain that to me.

As seen on I-News' 100 of Homer Simpson's Most Hilariously Hair-Brained Quotes

When you borrow something from your neighbour, always do it under the cover of darkness.

As seen on *Esquire*'s, "Homer Simpson: What I've Learned"

When I'm dead, I'm going to sleep. Oh, man, am I going to sleep.

As seen on I-News' 100 of Homer Simpson's Most Hilariously Hair-Brained Quotes

Lisa, if you don't like your job you don't strike. You just go in every day and do it really half-assed. That's the American way.

Homer *suggests there is more than one way to skin a cat!*

As seen on Screenrant's Best Quotes from *The Simpsons* (Season 6, Episode 21, "The PTA Disbands")

CHAPTER
TWO

BART'S
BEST
ONE-LINERS

Eternally trapped inside the body of a
10-year-old, Bart Simpson is *the enfant
terrible*. In the 1990s, Bart was the voice
of Generation X, a failure of the public
school system, but blessed with an ironic
sense of humour.

From education to politics, religion to
television, Bart schooled audiences
worldwide to question the motives of so-
called authority institutions and figures…
and told them to eat his shorts.

Viva la Bart!

66

Eat my shorts!

99

__Bart's__ dismissive barb to anything and almost everything…

Numerous episodes – as seen on Screenrant's Best Quotes from *The Simpsons*

"

Ay, caramba!

"

Bart's *go-to response for anything surprising or intriguing.*

Numerous episodes – as seen on Screenrant's Best Quotes from *The Simpsons*

In 1998, Bart Simpson was named as one of the "Most Influential People of the Century" by *TIME* magazine.

Lisa, you've got the brains and talent to go as far as you want, and when you do, I'll be right there to borrow money.

*Openly honest as ever, **Bart** imagines a future where his sister Lisa is the chief breadwinner.*

As seen on Screenrant's Best Quotes from *The Simpsons*

Martin: A blindfolded chimp with a pencil in his teeth has a better chance of passing this test than you do.
Bart: Thanks for the pep talk...

Bart's reputation in the education department goes before him…

As seen on Screenrant's Best Quotes from *The Simpsons* (Season 2, Episode 1, "Bart Gets an F")

"

Moe: Moe's Tavern, where the elite meet to drink.
Bart: Uh, yeah, hello. Is Mike there? Last name, Rotch?
Moe: Hold on, I'll check. Mike Rotch! Mike Rotch! Hey, has anybody seen Mike Rotch lately?

"

Bart's recurring torment of local bar owner Moe.

As seen on Simpsons.Fandom.com
(Season 2, Episode 22, "Blood Feud")

66

Moe: Hello, Moe's Tavern. Birthplace of the Rob Roy.

Bart: Is Seymour there? Last name, Butz.

Moe: Just a sec. Hey, is there a Butz here? Seymour Butz? Hey, everybody! I want a Seymour Butz!

99

Nobody excels in childish pranks more than the prince of child pranksters…

As seen on Simpsons.Fandom.com (Season 2, Episode 11, "One Fish, Two Fish, Blowfish, Blue Fish")

"

Bart: Hello? Is Homer there?

Moe: Homer who?

Bart: Homer … Sexual.

Moe: Wait one sec. Let me check. Uh, Homer Sexual? Uh, come on. Come on. One of you guys has gotta be Homer Sexual.

"

As seen on Screenrant's Best Quotes of *The Simpsons* (Season 2, Episode 14, "Principal Charming")

Matt Groening grew up in Portland, Oregon and says Springfield has much in common with his home city.

There are 29 Springfields dotted across the USA and Groening believed: "This will be cool; everyone will think it's their Springfield."

And they do!

❝

Milhouse: You shake it up, and it tells the future!

Bart: Really? Will I pass my English test? (shakes the ball)

Bart: 'Outlook not so good.' Wow, it does work!

❞

Bart sees no reason to disagree with Milhouse's prediction gadget.

As seen on Kidadl's 101 Best Simpsons Quotes (Season 3, Episode 23, "Bart's Friend Falls in Love")

There's a 4:30 in the morning now?

Bart Simpson – *not an early riser by habit…*

As seen on the *Telegraph's* Best Ever Simpsons Quotes
(Season 6, Episode 14, "Bart's Comet")

Everything changes when you get to the big one-o. Your legs start to go, candy doesn't taste as good anymore.

Bart *contemplates the downside of life as a 10-year-old...*

As seen on Kidadl's Best Simpsons Quotes (Season 3, Episode 1, "Stark Raving Dad")

66

Hey, cool, I'm dead.

99

*Typical response by **Bart** on learning of his own passing following an automobile accident – he recovers, of course…*

As seen on Den of Geek's Best Simpsons Quotes (Season 2, Episode 10, "Bart Gets Hit by a Car")

"

I think Grampa smells like that trunk in the garage where the bottom's all wet.

"

Bart – *never one to keep his observations in check – particularly when it concerns one particular elderly relative…*

As seen on the *Telegraph's* Best Simpsons Quotes (Season 2, Episode 17, "Old Money")

Mom, Dad, just so you don't hear any wild rumours, I'm being indicted for fraud in Australia.

***Bart** drops his parents a bombshell of continental proportions after making a random collect call Down Under and failing to hang up results in Australian government intervention.*

As seen on Simpsons.Fandom.com
(Season 6, Episode 16, "Bart vs. Australia")

"

If you don't watch the violence, you'll never get desensitized to it.

"

As seen on Kidadl's Best Simpsons Quotes
(Season 3, Episode 20, "Colonel Homer")

CHAPTER
THREE

THE VOICES OF REASON – MARGE AND LISA SIMPSON

Marge, the put-upon and devoted (but often disapproving) matriarch of the Simpsons, and Lisa, the nerdy and critical (but overlooked) eight-year-old daughter, are often the only rational voices left in Springfield, the essential counterpoint to the rest of the town's mob mentality.

For those who go diving for Marge's pearls of wisdom, and Lisa's liberal reasoning, enlightenment will be found.

It's Patty who chose a life of celibacy. Selma had celibacy thrust upon her.

Marge explains the differing reasons why her identical twin sisters have remained spinsters…

As seen on Screenrant's Best Quotes from *The Simpsons*

Homer, I like to think that I'm a patient, tolerant woman and that there was no line that you could cross that would make me stop loving you. But last night you didn't just cross that line, you threw up on it!

Marge *suggests Homer is walking on thin ice.*

As seen on Reddit's *Simpsons* Quotes for Every Day
(Season 2, Episode 20, "The War of the Simpsons")

Normally your father's crackpot schemes fizzle out as soon as he finds something good on TV. But this season…

Marge has seen most of this all before…

As seen on Screenrant's Best Quotes from *The Simpsons*
(Season 7, Episode 7, "King-Size Homer")

These are Homer's friends and family. They don't want him dead. They just want him to suffer.

Marge suggests a modicum of payback might be nice…

As seen on Reddit's *Simpsons* Quotes for Every Day (Season 14, Episode 6, "The Great Louse Detectives")

Since its debut as a standalone show on December 17, 1989, 732 episodes of the show have been broadcast.

It is the longest-running American animated series, longest-running American sitcom, and the longest-running American scripted prime-time television series, both in terms of seasons and number of episodes.

Oh, I've always wanted to use rosemary in something!

"

Quintessential **Marge Simpson.**

As seen on Simpsons.Fandom.com
(Season 11, Episode 21, "It's a Mad, Mad, Mad, Mad Marge")

You know, Homer, when I found out about this I went through a wide range of emotions. First, I was nervous, then anxious, then wary, then apprehensive, then kinda sleepy, then worried, and then concerned. But now I realize that being a spaceman is something you have to do.

When dealing a husband like Homer, **Marge** *reaches this inevitable conclusion.*

As seen on Screenrant's Best Quotes from *The Simpsons* (Season 5, Episode 15, "Deep Space Homer")

Lisa's growing up. It's a really complicated time in a girl's life from age eight to… Actually, all the rest of the way.

*More worldly wisdom from **Marge.***

As seen on Screenrant's Best Quotes from *The Simpsons* (Season 25, Episode 20, "Brick Like Me")

I don't mind if you pee in the shower, but only if you're taking a shower.

*Life with Homer is never easy for **Marge**...*

As seen on Reddit's Simpsons Quotes for Every Day (Season 21, Episode 14, "Postcards from the Wedge")

I've been so bored since we've moved here, I've found myself drinking a glass of wine every day. I know doctors say you should drink a glass and a half, but I just can't drink that much.

Marge – *a woman who knows her limits!*

As seen on Screenrant's Best Quotes from *The Simpsons* (Season 8, Episode 2, "You Only Move Twice")

66

You should listen to your heart, and not the voices inside your head.

99

*Sound advice we can all follow from **Marge**...*

As seen on Bust.com's Marge Simpson's Best Quotes
(Season 5, Episode 20, "The Boy Who Knew Too Much")

My interests include music, science, justice, animals, shapes, feelings...

Lisa Simpson *outlines her highbrow hobbies and likes.*

As seen on Reddit's *Simpsons* Quotes for Everyday (Season 14, Episode 16, "Scuse Me While I Miss the Sky")

I am tired of being a corporate shill! From now on, I will speak out against the evils in society from dog-napping to cigarettes!

Lisa Simpson's *journey to the White House starts here…*

As seen on Simpsons.Fandom.com
(Season 4, Episode 4, "Lisa the Beauty Queen")

66

There's a lot more to it than that, Bart. I don't just babysit. I sell peace of mind for a dollar an hour. Two dollars after 9 o'clock.

Lisa speaks for babysitters the world over...

As seen on Simpsons.Fandom.com
(Season 8, Episode 17, "My Sister, My Sitter")

It's amazing how I can feel sorry for you and hate you at the same time. I'm sure there's a German word for it.

*If there is, **Lisa** will find it…*

As seen on Reddit's *Simpsons* Quotes for Every Day (Season 22, Episode 7, "How Munched is that Birdie in the Window?")

66

Look, Dad! I made a modern studio apartment for my Malibu Stacey Doll. This is the kitchen. This is where she prints her weekly feminist newsletter... dad! You're not listening to me!

99

The one and only... **Lisa Simpson.**

As seen on Simpsons.Fandom.com
(Season 3, Episode 14, "Lisa the Greek")

They want sentiment?
I'll pump 'em so full of sap
they'll have to blow their nose
with a pancake!

Lisa Simpson – *wise – and cynical –
beyond her years…*

As seen on Simpsons.Fandom.com
(Season 9, Episode 21, "Girly Edition")

❝

I learned that beneath my goody two-shoes lies some very dark socks.

❞

Lisa *admits to her steely resolve in her own, unique style.*

As seen on Simpsons.Fandom.com
(Season 19, Episode 14, "Dial 'N' For Nerder")

I'm proud of you, Mom. You're like Christopher Columbus. You discovered something millions of people knew about before you.

Lisa *congratulates Marge on her early success surfing the web.*

As seen on Simpsons.Fandom.com
(Season 18, Episode 17, "Marge Gamer")

❝

Mom, look, I found something more fun than complaining!

❞

Lisa falls in love with horse riding…

As seen on Simpsons.Fandom.com (Season 7, Episode 14,
"Scenes from the Class Struggle in Springfield")

"

Mom, romance is dead. It was acquired by Hallmark and Disney in a hostile takeover, homogenized, and sold off piece by piece.

"

Lisa affirms her role as the smartest and sharpest Simpson with her observation of a commercialized America.

As seen on Simpsons.Fandom.com
(Season 6, Episode 3, "Another Simpsons Clip Show")

You mean those leagues where parents push their kids into vicious competition to compensate for their own failed dreams of glory?

__Lisa's__ gym teacher encourages her to join out-of-school clubs to improve her fitness – but she has reservations.

As seen on Screenrant's Best Quotes from *The Simpsons*

Well, I'm going to be a famous jazz musician. I've got it all figured out. I'll be unappreciated in my own country, but my gutsy blues stylings will electrify the French. I'll avoid the horrors of drug abuse, but I do plan to have several torrid love affairs, and I may or may not die young. I haven't decided.

Lisa's *meticulously mapped out path to eternal coolness!*

As seen on Screenrant's Best Quotes from *The Simpsons* (Season 3, Episode 18, "Separate Vocations")

> **"**
> I think you need Skinner, Bart. Everybody needs a nemesis.
> **"**

Lisa gives her brother some hard truths about his principal.

As seen on Kidadl's Best Simpsons Quotes (Season 5, Episode 19, "Sweet Seymour Skinner's Baadasssss Song")

....

CHAPTER
FOUR

FAMILY LIFE

To their critics, the Simpsons clan embody the decline of wholesome values.

To their fans, *The Simpsons* is a window into America's soul, as beautiful and broken as the Monorail.

If the Simpsons teach us anything, however, it's that family matters most, no matter how crazy, lazy or amazing they may be!

Homer: I'm sorry, Marge, but sometimes I think we're the worst family in town.
Marge: Maybe we should move to a larger community.

Marge's pragmatic solution to her family's reputation in Springfield.

As seen on Simpsons.Fandom.com

Two-times Emmy
award-winning composer
Danny Elfman took just
two days to compose the
show's theme song.

Marge: Homer, I really appreciate you making dinner, but this food tastes a little strange.

Lisa: It hurts my teeth.

Homer: That's because I've loaded it with sugar! Marge, our ship has come in! I found five hundred pounds of sugar in the forest that I'm going to sell directly to the consumer!

All for a low, low price of $1 per pound.

Marge: But the grocery store sells sugar for thirty-five cents a pound.

Lisa: And it doesn't have nails and broken glass in it.

Homer: Those are prizes! (eating) Ooh, a blasting cap.

"

As seen on Simpsons.Fandom.com
(Season 6, Episode 2, "Lisa's Rival")

"

Homer: Son, if you can look me in the eye and say you didn't take the collection money, that's all I need.

Bart: I didn't take it.

Homer: Why you little... How can you look me in the eye and lie like that?!

"

As seen on Screenrant's Best Quotes from *The Simpsons* (Season 6, Episode 7, "Bart's Girlfriend")

66

Marge: I don't think it's a good idea to be driving around in a car you built yourself.
Homer: (Building a car out of a mattress) Okay, Marge, either you can stand there and complain, or you can get started knitting me those seatbelts.

99

As seen on Screenrant's Best Quotes from *The Simpsons* (Season 9, Episode 1, "The City of New York vs. Homer Simpson")

Lisa: Mom, are those rabbits dead?

Marge: No, no, Lisa, they're just sleeping, upside down... and inside out.

As seen on Screenrant's Best Quotes from *The Simpsons* (Season 9, Episode 1, "The City of New York vs. Homer Simpson")

"

Homer: Marge, you've been out there all morning.

Marge: So?

Homer: So, lying on the couch and eating stuff isn't the same if you aren't around to see it.

"

As seen on I-News' Best *Simpsons* Quotes (Season 10, Episode 15, "Marge Simpson in: Screaming Yellow Honkers")

Bart: I'll have the brain burger with extra pus, please.

Marge: Bart!

Homer: Eyeball stew.

Marge: Homer! We just got here and already I'm mortified beyond belief by your embarrassing behaviour.

Bart: I was just ordering a cheeseburger, Mom. They have violent names for everything here.

Marge: Oh, I see. All right. I'll have the baby guts.
Waiter: Lady, you disgust me.
Lisa: Mom, that's veal.

"

The Simpsons visit to Itchy and Scratchy Land – a theme park dedicated to bloodthirsty mouse and cat characters from Bart's favourite animated series.

As seen on Screenrant's Best Quotes from *The Simpsons* (Season 6, Episode 4, "Itchy and Scratchy Land")

Marge: Homey, are you really going
to ignore Grampa for the rest of your life?

Homer: Of course not, Marge, just for the rest of his life. He said I was an accident...he didn't want to have me.

Marge: You didn't want to have Bart.

Homer: I know, but you're never supposed to tell the child.
Marge: You tell Bart all the time! You told him this morning.
Homer: But when I do it, it's cute.

99

As seen on Screenrant's Best Quotes from *The Simpsons* (Season 6, Episode 10, "Grandpa vs Sexual Inadequacy")

Marge: Homer, is this the way you pictured married life?
Homer: Yeah, pretty much, except we drove round in a van solving mysteries.

Homer admits he expected something a little extra after he tied the knot with Marge...

The *Telegraph's* 40 Best Simpsons Quotes
(Season 8, Episode 6, "A Milhouse Divided")

Homer: We're proud of you, Boy.
Bart: Thanks, Dad. Part of this D-minus belongs to God.

Bart's efforts in class sees him achieve his best grade yet – much to Homer's pride.

The *Telegraph's* 40 Best *Simpsons* Quotes
(Season 2, Episode 1, "Bart Gets an F")

66

Lisa: I'm going to become a vegetarian.
Homer: Does that mean you're not going to eat any pork?
Lisa: Yes.
Homer: Bacon?
Lisa: Yes, Dad.
Homer: Ham?

Lisa: Dad all those meats come from the same animal.
Homer: Right, Lisa, some wonderful, magical animal!

"

Homer tries to get his head around what a vegetarian actually can and can't eat…

As seen on the *Telegraph's* 40 Best *Simpsons* Quotes

66

Lisa: You promised to take us to the lake.

Homer: I promise you kids lots of things. That's what makes me such a good father.

Lisa: Actually, keeping promises would make you a good father.

Homer: No, that would make me a great father.

99

As seen on Screenrant's Best Quotes from *The Simpsons* (Season 10, Episode 5, "When You Dish Upon a Star")

"

Lisa: What do you say to a boy to let him know you're not interested?
Marge: Well, honey, when I...
Homer: Let me handle this, Marge; I've heard 'em all. I like you as a friend... I think we should see other people... I no speak English...
Lisa: I get the idea.

"

Lisa always takes Homer's fatherly advice on board!

As seen on Screenrant's Best Quotes from *The Simpsons* (Season 4, Episode 15, "I Love Lisa")

CHAPTER
FIVE

THE WEIRD AND WONDERFUL WORLD OF SPRINGFIELD

Springfield – a place like no other.

A town full of misfits, oddballs and everything in between.

Where is it? Nobody knows, but it's often described as "Anytown, USA".

Meet its unforgettable and hilarious inhabitants…

The Simpsons creator
Matt Groening got
many of the characters'
surnames from real streets
in his hometown
of Portland, Oregon.

66

Barney: Hello, my name is Barney Gumble, and I'm an alcoholic.

Lisa: Mr Gumble, this is a girl scouts meeting.

Barney: Is it, or is it you girls can't admit that you have a problem?

99

Resident Springfield alcoholic Barney Gumble mistakes girl scouts for an AA meeting…

As seen on Screenrant's Best Quotes from *The Simpsons* (Season 6, Episode 18, "A Star Is Burns")

Shoplifting is a victimless crime. Like punching someone in the dark.

*School bully **Nelson Muntz** justifies one crime by comparing it to another.*

From Screenrant's Best Quotes from *The Simpsons*

This anonymous clan of slack-jawed troglodytes has cost me the election. And yet, if I were to have them killed, I would be the one to go to jail. That's democracy for you.

*The eternally bitter multi-millionaire **Mr Burns** sees his bid to become Governor and save his unsafe nuclear power plant from being closed sabotaged by Marge Simpson.*

Screenrant's Best Quotes from *The Simpsons* (Season 2, Episode 4, "Two Cars in Every Garage and Three Eyes on Every Fish")

> **66**
>
> **Moe:** Homer, lighten up!
> You're making Happy Hour
> bitterly ironic.
>
> **99**

*Moe Szyslak, proprietor of Moe's Tavern,
with a typically acerbic observation.*

The *Telegraph's* 40 Best *Simpsons* Quotes

"

Comic Book Guy: That is a rare photo of Sean Connery signed by Roger Moore; it is worth one hundred and fifty dollars.

Milhouse: What can I get for seventy-five cents?

Comic Book Guy: Ugh, you may purchase this charming Hamburglar adventure, a child has already solved the jumble using crayons. The answer is 'fries'.

"

As seen on Simpsons.Fandom.com
(Season 7, Episode 22, "Short Films About Springfield")

Moe: Barney, remember when I said I'd have to send away to NASA to calculate your bar tab?

Barney: Yeah, we all had a good laugh, Moe.

Moe: The results came back today. You owe me 70 billion dollars.

Barney: Mmmph!?

Moe: No, wait wait, wait, that's for the Voyager spacecraft. Your tab's 14 billion dollars.
Barney: Uh, alls I got is 2,000 bucks.
Moe: Well, that's halfway there.

99

Moe's maths drastically reduces Barney's sizeable tab…

As seen on Simpsons.Fandom.com

Your theory of a donut-shaped universe is intriguing, Homer. I may have to steal it.

*Guest star **Stephen Hawking** utters a line only Matt Groening could have come up with!*

As seen on Screenrant's Best Quotes from *The Simpsons* (Season 10, Episode 22, "They Saved Lisa's Brain")

Lisa, you don't spend ten years as a homicidal maniac without learning a few things about dynamite.

Lisa's question regarding Bob's knowledge of explosives receives a typically erudite answer from Springfield's occasional madman (voiced by Kelsey Grammer).

As seen on Screenrant's 10 Best Sideshow Bob Quotes

Can I make my famous mimosa?
A little sparkling water in a glass
full of regular water?

Ned Flanders – *the long-suffering but good-natured neighbour of the Simpsons.*

As seen on I-News' Best *Simpsons* Quotes
(Season 26, Episode 21, "Bull-E")

> **"**
>
> # Oh, loneliness and cheeseburgers are a dangerous mix.
>
> **"**

Comic Book Guy – *AKA Jeff Albertson – professional nerd and owner of the Springfield comic book store, ponders the weighty issues of bachelor life.*

As seen on Reddit's Simpsons Quotes for Every Day

66

Vendor: Hot dogs, get your hot dogs!
Homer: I'll take one.
Marge: What, do you follow my husband around to sell him hot dogs?
Vendor: Lady, he's putting my kids through college.

99

Marge gets an insight into some unique Springfield sales techniques – at least those involving her husband...

As seen on the *Telegraph's* 40 Best *Simpsons* Quotes

Although kissing you would be like kissing some divine ashtray, that's not what I had in mind.

Selma – one of Marge's twin sisters – and
Sideshow Bob *meet through a prison pen-pal scheme – but Bob's intentions are not what they seem...*

As seen on Screenrant's 10 Best Sideshow Bob Quotes

I've been called ugly, pug ugly, fugly, pug fugly, but never ugly ugly.

Moe Szyslak *reveals how his "unique" looks have caused various reactions over the years.*

As seen on the *Telegraph's* 40 Best *Simpsons* Quotes

66

Last night's *Itchy & Scratchy* was, without a doubt, the worst episode ever. Rest assured I was on the internet within minutes registering my disgust throughout the world.

99

Comic Book Guy *responds with disgust to the latest episode of the long-running and ultra-violent kids' cartoon* Itchy & Scratchy.

As seen on the *Telegraph's* 40 Best *Simpsons* Quotes

Bless the grocer for this wonderful meat, the middleman who jacked up the price, and let's not forget the humane but determined boys at the slaughterhouse.

Ned Flanders' *wholesome and informed view of just about... everything.*

As seen on Reddit's *Simpsons* Quotes for Every Day
(Season 5, Episode 16, "Homer Loves Flanders")

Why me, Lord? Where have I gone wrong? I've always been nice to people! I don't drink or dance or swear! I've even kept kosher, just to be on the safe side. I've done everything the Bible says; even the stuff that contradicts the other stuff! What more could I do?

Ned Flanders *asks his God for answers after the hurricane strike.*

As seen on Screenrant's Best Quotes from *The Simpsons* (Season 8, Episode 8, "Hurricane Neddy")

On March 3, 2021, the series was announced to have been renewed for seasons 33 and 34, which were later confirmed to have 22 episodes each, increasing the episode count from 706 to 750.

The 34th season premiered on September 25, 2022.

66

Now what can I ding dong diddly do for you?

99

*One of **Ned Flanders'** many hokey catchphrases.*

As seen on Screenrant's Best Quotes from *The Simpsons* (Season 8, Episode 8, "Hurricane Neddy")

Convenience forever, freshness never!

Apu Nahasapeemapetilon, *Springfield's 7-11 store proprietor and champion of mini-markets across the world.*

As seen on TV Fanatic's Best *Simpsons* Quotes

I'm not the kind of dad who, y'know, does things, or says stuff, or looks at you. But the love is there!

Krusty *has as close to a Kodak moment as he'll get with his daughter Sophie.*

As seen on Screenrant's Best Quotes from *The Simpsons* (Season 12, Episode 3, "Insane Clown Poppy")

One of creator Matt Groening's original ideas was to reveal that Krusty the Clown was actually Homer Simpson – the reason why they look so similar – but the idea was eventually shelved.

Homer gave me a kidney – it wasn't his, I didn't need it, and it came postage due – but still, a lovely gesture.

Krusty the Clown

As seen on Screenrant's Best Quotes from _The Simpsons_

"

If you get hungry in the middle of the night, there's an open beer in the fridge.

"

*Springfield's professional drunk **Barney Gumble** – guaranteed to always have a beer at hand if needed.*

As seen on *The Simpsons* Forever Best Quotes

We home-school 'em. I teach the big ones and the big ones teach the little ones. But no one ever taught me, which makes the whole thing just an exercise in futility.

Cletus Spuckler – *Springfield's very own poor white trash representative, parent, and loveable dimwit.*

As seen on *The Simpsons* Forever Best Quotes

What makes a man endanger his job, and, yes, even his life, by asking me for money?

Mr Burns – *the miserly millionaire of Springfield and all-round misery guts.*

As seen on Kidadl's Best Mr Burns Quotes

I guess this is the end. I just wish
I'd spent more time at the office.

Mr Burns – *guaranteed to flip even the best
deathbed lines on their head.*

As seen on *The Simpsons* Forever Best Quotes

The Simpsons takes place in the fictional American town of Springfield – though is not based on any one town in particular.

Springfield's geography contains coastlines, deserts, vast farmland, tall mountains, or whatever the storyline requires.

> 66
>
> **Homer:** Where are we going, sir?
> **Mr Burns:** To create a new and better world!
> **Homer:** If it's on the way, could you drop me off at my house?
>
> 99

Mr Burns decides to run for Governor amid the threat of bankruptcy.

As seen on Kidadl's Best *Simpsons* Quotes (Season 2, Episode 4, "Two Cars in Every Garage and Three Eyes on Every Fish")

"

Bart: You did it, Homer, you saved me from the bullies, you're the coolest kid I've ever met.
Milhouse: What about me?
Bart: You're in the top hundred.
Milhouse: Booyah!
Bart: Now you're not.

"

As seen on TV Fanatic's Best *Simpsons* Character Quotes

66

Grampa: That's Mock Rickly,
my old Air Force buddy.

Bart: You said you were in
the Army.

Lisa: You said you were in
the Navy.

Grampa: That's the kind of
mix up that used to happen
when I was in the Marines.

99

Lisa and *Bart* suspect their Grandpa may be
exaggerating his military background…

As seen on Simpsons.Fandom.com

CHAPTER
SIX

THE BEST OF TREEHOUSE OF HORROR

From lampooning celebrities, spoofing movie or TV scenes, or satirizing political news, the Treehouse of Horror episodes are our yearly reminders of how important it is to poke those in need of a good prod, and to frighten viewers, not by jump scares, but by asking them to admit their collective cultural demons and villains – and to shoo them away with pitchforks until they become someone else's problems.

"

Today he's drinking people's blood. Tomorrow he could be smoking.

"

Marge *raises concerns about where Bart's vampire-like behaviour could lead.*

As seen on Simpsons.Fandom.com
(Season 2, Episode 3, "Treehouse of Horror")

Why is it when a woman is confident and powerful, they call her a witch?

Lisa asks a not-unreasonable question…

As seen on Simpsons.Fandom.com
(Season 20, Episode 4, "Treehouse of Horror XIX")

There goes the last lingering thread of my heterosexuality.

*Marge's sister **Patty** delivers a killer line as Homer races naked through the house trying to escape a demonic Krusty doll.*

As seen on Simpsons.Fandom.com ("Treehouse of Horror III")

Bart: I've got a story so scary
you'll wet your pants.
Grampa: Too late.

As seen on Screenrant's Best Quotes from *The Simpsons*
(Season 4, "Treehouse of Horror III")

Lisa: Mom! Mom! You've gotta help! They're cooking kids in the school cafeteria!

Marge: Listen, kids. You're eight and ten years old now. I can't be fighting all your battles for you.

Bart: But, Mom!

Marge: No buts. You march right back to that school, look them straight in the eye and say, don't eat me.

"

As seen on Reddit's *Simpsons* Quotes for Every Day

Marge: (over radio) Hello, police? This is Marge Simpson. My husband is on a murderous rampage. Over.

Chief Wiggum: Oh, well thank God that's over. I was worried there for a second.

As seen on Simpsons.Fandom.com
(Season 6, Episode 6, "Treehouse of Horror V")

Bart! Stop pestering Satan.

Marge's *motherly advice as her son's devilish sense of humour threatens grave consequences…*

As seen on Reddit's *Simpsons* Quotes for Every Day (Season 7, Episode 10, "Simpsons 138th Episode Spectacular")

Mr Burns: This house has quite a long and colourful history. It was built on an ancient Indian burial ground, and was the setting of satanic rituals, witch burnings, and five John Denver Christmas Specials.
Homer: (shudders) John Denver.

As seen on Reddit's *Simpsons* Quotes for Every Day

Don't eat me. I have a wife and kids. Eat them.

Homer Simpson *– the man who invented self-preservation!*

As seen on the *Telegraph's* Best 40 *Simpsons* Quotes (Season 8, Episode 10, "Treehouse of Horror VII")

CHAPTER
SEVEN

BEER AND DONUTS

HOMER'S BEST ONE-LINERS

Mmm, beer and donuts.

For more than 30 years, and 730 episodes, an entire generation of Americans' sense of humour has been shaped by this Duff-downing, donut-dipping D'oh boy.

Even when *The Simpsons* is no longer on our screens, Homer's most quotable one-liners will live on, teaching new generations of fathers, sons, and men that stupid risks are what make life worth living.

66

Books are useless! I only ever read one book, *To Kill a Mockingbird,* and it gave me absolutely no insight on how to kill mockingbirds!

99

__Homer__ reveals the reasons behind his decision not to continue reading books – classics or otherwise – after his disappointing experience.

The *Telegraph's* 40 Best *Simpsons* Quotes
(Season 15, Episode 10, "Diatribe of a Mad Housewife")

66

Homer: Ooh, Mama! This is finally, really happening. After years of disappointment with get-rich-quick schemes, I know I'm gonna get rich with this scheme... and quick!

99

As seen on the *Telegraph's* Best 40 *Simpsons* Quotes

It's not easy to juggle a pregnant wife and a troubled child, but somehow I managed to fit in eight hours of TV a day.

Homer *reveals the secret of multi-tasking…*

As seen on the *Telegraph's* 40 Best *Simpsons* Quotes

If *The Flintstones* has taught us anything, it's that pelicans can be used to mix cement.

As seen on the *Telegraph's* Best 40 *Simpsons* Quotes
(Season 11, Episode 15, "Missionary Impossible")

Matt Groening
named Homer after
his own father,
Homer Groening.

"

Oh, I have three kids and no money. Why can't I have no kids and three money?

"

As seen on the *Telegraph's* Best 40 *Simpsons* Quotes
(Season 18, Episode 19, "Crook and Ladder")

Spider-Pig, Spider-Pig, does whatever a Spider-Pig does. Can he swing from a web? No, he can't, he's a pig, look out, he is a Spider-Pig!

Homer's love for his pet pig results in a passable Spiderman impression – with limitations.

As seen on Screenrant's Best Quotes from *The Simpsons* (Season 28, Episode 11, "Pork & Burns")

A gun is not a weapon,
it's a tool, like a hammer or a
screwdriver or an alligator.

As seen on Screenrant's Best Quotes from *The Simpsons*

I thought I had an appetite for destruction, but all I wanted was a club sandwich.

As seen on Screenrant's Best Quotes from *The Simpsons*

I'll make the money by selling one of my livers… I can get by with one.

As seen on Screenrant's Best Quotes from *The Simpsons*

Marge, you being a cop makes you the man! Which makes me the woman – and I have no interest in that, besides occasionally wearing the underwear, which as we discussed, is strictly a comfort thing.

As seen on I-News' Best *Simpsons* Quotes

66

Vampires are make-believe,
just like elves, gremlins
and Eskimos.

99

As seen on I-News' Best *Simpsons* Quotes

That's it! You people have stood in my way long enough. I'm going to clown college!

Homer *finally commits to a lifelong ambition…*

As seen on the *Telegraph's* 40 Best *Simpsons* Quotes

66
Kids, just because I don't care doesn't mean I'm not listening.
99

*Honesty is always the best policy for **Homer**...*

As seen on I-News' Best *Simpsons* Quotes
(Season 2, Episode 7, "Bart vs. Thanksgiving")

Operator! Give me the number for 911!

As seen on Simpsons.Fandom.com
(Season 2, Episode 7, "Bart vs. Thanksgiving")

66

Marge, you're my wife of ten years and I love you, but I must observe the teachings of this man I just met tonight.

99

As seen on Simpsons.Fandom.com
(Season 26, Episode 13, "Walking Big and Tall")

For once, maybe someone will call me 'sir' without adding, 'you're making a scene.'

Homer *contemplates life as a Springfield Country Club member – what could possibly go wrong?*

As seen on Simpsons.Fandom.com (Season 7, Episode 14, "Scenes from a Class Struggle in Springfield")

> 66
>
> All my life, I've had one dream:
> to achieve my many goals.
>
> 99

As seen on Reddit's *Simpsons* Quotes for Every Day
(Season 14, Episode 15, "C.E. D'OH")

"

Simpson! Homer Simpson! He's the greatest guy in his-tor-y … from the town of Springfield! He's about to hit a chestnut tree!

"

Homer cannibalizes the Flintstones *theme ahead of wrecking the family car.*

As seen on Reddit's *Simpsons* Quotes for Every Day
(Season 4, Episode 12, "Marge vs. the Monorail")

"

I saw this movie about a bus that had to speed around a city, keeping its speed over fifty, and if its speed dropped, it would explode! I think it was called, 'The Bus That Couldn't Slow Down'.

"

Homer's *attempt to recall the title of the movie* Speed *ends with typically hilarious results.*

As seen on Reddit's *Simpsons* Quotes for Every Day (Season 7, Episode 10, "The Springfield Files")

66

You'll have to speak up: I'm wearing a towel.

99

As seen on the *Telegraph's* Best 40 *Simpsons* Quotes
(Season 3, Episode 17, "Homer at the Bat")

> **"**
> Marge, you know it's rude to talk when my mouth is full.
> **"**

As seen on the *Telegraph's* Best 40 *Simpsons* Quotes

Old people don't need companionship. They need to be isolated and studied so it can be determined what nutrients they have that might be extracted for our personal use.

As seen on Screenrant's Best Quotes from *The Simpsons*

> **"**
> Look. Moe, the least you can let
> me do is anything I want.
> **"**

As seen on I-News' 100 of Homer Simpson's Most
Hilariously Hair-Brained Quotes

Overdue book? This is the biggest frame-up since OJ! Wait a minute. Blood in the Bronco. The cuts on his hands. Those Jay Leno monologues. Oh my god, he did it!

As seen on Screenrant's Best Quotes from *The Simpsons*

66

Stupidity got us into this mess,
and stupidity will get us out.

99

As seen on Screenrant's Best Quotes from *The Simpsons*

We can outsmart those dolphins. Don't forget – we invented computers, leg warmers, bendy straws, peel-and-eat shrimp, the glory hole, and the pudding cup.

As seen on I-News' 100 of Homer Simpson's Most Hilariously Hair-Brained Quotes

66

If it doesn't have Siamese twins
in a jar, it is not a fair.

99

As seen on I-News' 100 of Homer Simpson's Most
Hilariously Hair-Brained Quotes

In the 1975 movie,
Day of the Locust,
Donald Sutherland played
a character named
Homer Simpson.

Sutherland's world came
full circle when he
appeared in a *Simpsons*
episode called "Lisa the
Iconoclast".

I'm like that guy who single-handedly built the rocket and flew to the moon. What was his name? Apollo Creed?

As seen on I-News' 100 of Homer Simpson's Most Hilariously Hair-Brained Quotes

Roads are just a suggestion, Marge. Just like pants.

As seen on I-News' 100 of Homer Simpson's Most Hilariously Hair-Brained Quotes

66

Volunteering is for suckers. Did you know that volunteers don't even get paid for the stuff they do?

99

As seen on I-News' 100 of Homer Simpson's Most Hilariously Hair-Brained Quotes

"

I'm normally not a praying man, but if you're up there, please save, me Superman.

"

As seen on I-News' 100 of Homer Simpson's Most Hilariously Hair-Brained Quotes

"

Okay. I'm not going to kill you, but I'm going to tell you three things that will haunt you the rest of your days. You ruined your father. You crippled your family. And baldness is hereditary!

"

As seen on I-News' 100 of Homer Simpson's Most Hilariously Hair-Brained Quotes

All right, brain. You don't like me, and I don't like you, but let's just do this and I can get back to killing you with beer.

As seen on I-News' 100 of Homer Simpson's Most Hilariously Hair-Brained Quotes

> **"**
> I'm a white male, age 18 to 49. Everyone listens to me, no matter how dumb my suggestions are.
> **"**

As seen on I-News' 100 of Homer Simpson's Most Hilariously Hair-Brained Quotes

Mmm… donuts.

Homer's *go-to response whenever he sees the American delicacy.*

Numerous episodes – as seen on I-News' 100 of Homer Simpson's Most Hilariously Hair-Brained Quotes